on duty

Life as an Air Force Fighter Pilot

Robert C. Kennedy

HIGH interest books

Children's Press
A Division of Grolier Publishing
New York / London / Hong Kong / Sydney
Danbury, Connecticut

Book Design: Nelson Sa
Contributing Editor: Mark Beyer

Photo Credits: Cover, pp. 5, 7, 9, 10 © Index Stock Photography, Inc.; p. 12 ©
Corbis; pp. 15, 19 © /Corbis; pp. 20, 23 © George Hall/Corbis; p. 25 © Index
Stock Photography, Inc.; p. 28 © Corbis; p. 30 © Leif Skoogfors/Corbis; p. 32 ©
George Hall/Corbis; p. 35 © Corbis; pp. 37, 39, 41 © Index Stock
Photography, Inc.

Visit Children's Press on the Internet at:
http://publishing.grolier.com

Cataloging-in-Publication Data

Kennedy, Robert C.
    Life as an Air Force fighter pilot / by Robert C. Kennedy.
      p. cm. – (On duty)
    Includes bibliographical references and index.
    Summary: This book discusses Air Force officer training and requirements,
      the specialized training of Air Force fighter pilots, and the fighter pilot
      weapons that are used today.
    ISBN 0-516-23345-9 (lib. bdg.) – ISBN 0-516-23545-1 (pbk.)
    1. Fighter plane combat—United States—Juvenile literature. 2. Fighter
      pilots—United States—Juvenile literature. 3. United States. Air Force—
      Military life—Juvenile literature.
    [1. Fighter pilots. 2. United States. Air Force] I. Title. II. Series.
    UG703.K45 2000   00-040505
    358.4—dc21

CONTENTS

Introduction

The first airplanes were used in war during World War I (1914–1918). U.S. Army Signal Corps soldiers flew two-winged airplanes (biplanes) against the Germans. These airplanes were slow and not capable of doing much fighting. At first, the Signal Corps pilots watched enemy armies as they moved on the ground. From the air, pilots saw for long distances and easily flew over enemy territory. They reported what they spotted to U.S. headquarters.

Soon, however, Signal Corps pilots fought German airplanes in the skies. Fighter pilots were needed to battle enemy fighter planes. Groups of pilots were formed, called squadrons. These pilots began to learn how to fight air battles. Air battles were fought using machine guns connected to the front of the planes. These air battles were called dogfights because the planes circled each other while they were close. They shot at each other until

Thousands of airplanes were built for war in World War I (1914–1918).

either one pilot killed the other, or one plane was too shot up to fly. All of the armies fighting in the war realized that the airplane was a deadly weapon.

5

During World War II (1939–1945), the Army, Navy, and Marines used planes to fight some battles. The U.S. Air Force had not yet been formed. All of the pilots were specially trained in combat flying. They flew thousands of missions throughout the war.

Following the war, President Harry Truman understood the importance of military airpower. In 1947, the U.S. Department of Defense created the Air Force. Today, the Air Force is used more than any other branch of service during armed conflict around the world. This is because a single fighter pilot is able to do a great deal of damage to the enemy from thousands of feet in the air. Today's Air Force fighter pilot flies the most modern planes, and uses the most deadly weapons. Enemies fear U.S. Air Force fighter pilots because they are the best at what they do.

The look of the Air Force fighter pilot has changed since the days of biplanes and propellers.

The Air Force Fighter Pilot

WHO THEY ARE

Fighter pilots are a special breed. Their love of flying seems to overtake their fear of dying. Rest assured, fighter pilots are always in great danger. However, pilots learn to manage their fear. They also keep in mind an old saying: "There are bold pilots and old pilots but there are no old, bold pilots."

WHAT THEY DO

Air Force fighter pilots are based both in the United States and many foreign countries. Overseas bases are in countries such as England, Germany, Japan, Korea and many others.

Fighter pilots have a mission to protect both U.S. and allied (friendly) bases. To do that, they fly the most modern aircraft in the world.

Today's fighter pilots fly jets that are high-tech weapons.

LIFE AS AN AIR FORCE FIGHTER PILOT

These aircraft include the F-111, F-117A Nighthawk (stealth fighter), F-15 Eagle, F-16 Fighting Falcon, and the A-10/OA-10 Thunderbolt II. Fighter pilots must know the capabilities of their own aircraft and all the weapons they carry. They also must know the abilities of their enemy and that country's aircraft and weapons.

To defeat the enemy, pilots spend countless hours in flight simulators (machines that let a

pilot practice flying using video screens), fighting each other in fake air battles. Pilots practice dogfighting skills against other pilots. They use the same types of targeting systems as those found on the actual aircraft. When fighter pilots are in their planes, whether on patrol or flying a mission, they know what to expect.

ENTERING THE AIR FORCE AS AN OFFICER

A person entering Air Force officer training must be between twenty and twenty-eight years old. On completing the training, a recruit earns the rank (level) of second lieutenant (lowest grade of officer). Although women may serve as Air Force officers, they may not be fighter pilots. This is because fighter pilots are in combat units. By law, women cannot be in combat units. A person has three options by which he or she can become a commissioned (elected) Air Force officer.

Fighter pilots train using flight simulators.

11

Air Force Reserve Officers Training Corps (AFROTC)

The Air Force Reserve Officers Training Corps (AFROTC) pays for a recruit's college tuition and other benefits. High school graduates can get four-year scholarships. Graduates of AFROTC earn a Bachelor of Science degree and a reserve (held back for emergency) commission as a second lieutenant. After graduation, recruits take fifty-three weeks of training. This training includes how to command people, create budgets (use money), and learn military tactics (ways to fight).

Officer Training School (OTS)

The Officer Training School (OTS) is for people who already have a four-year college degree. Recruits must be between the ages of twenty and twenty-seven. Recruits attend a twelve-week school at Maxwell Air Force Base (AFB) in Alabama. Recruits who graduate receive a reserve commission as a second lieutenant.

U.S. Air Force Academy

High school seniors may apply for an appointment to the Air Force Academy in Colorado Springs, Colorado. Contact the U.S. Air Force Academy and your state senators and representatives for help. A graduate earns a Bachelor of Science degree and a reserve commission as a second lieutenant. However, Academy graduates are the main source for regular commissions, because they are needed by the Air Force. So, a reserve commission from the Academy could turn into a regular commission before long.

The U.S. Air Force Academy is located in Chapel, Colorado.

13

LIFE AS AN AIR FORCE FIGHTER PILOT

Another advantage to Academy training is that many airmanship courses are offered. Recruits who want to be pilots need to learn all they can about airplanes and flying. Recruits take courses from sailplane (small trainer) flight training to Federal Aviation Administration (FAA) instrument rating (ability to fly and land a jet using electronic gauges). The airmanship courses also include gliders, precision flight training, and both free-fall and advanced parachute training. These courses can't ensure a recruit's acceptance for fighter pilot training. But they certainly give a recruit an advantage over the competition.

ENTERING THE AIR FORCE AS AN ENLISTED PERSON

There were many enlisted pilots in the old Signal Corps and Army Air Corps. Now all fighter pilots have to be officers. However, enlisting does not prevent a recruit from becoming an officer. Once a recruit becomes an officer, he or

Pilots learn how to fly jets using trainers. When they are experienced flyers, they move up to the latest fighter planes used today.

she can become a fighter pilot. Any of these programs allow enlistees to finish their educations and earn reserve commissions as second lieutenants:

- Airman education and commission program (AECP)
- Scholarships for outstanding airmen to ROTC (SOAR)
- Airman scholarship and commissioning program (ASCP)

Fighter pilots must be young. Make sure you complete all your educational goals soon after enlistment.

HOW THE AIR FORCE IS ORGANIZED

The U.S. Department of Defense commands all military forces. U.S. military forces include the Department of the Army, Department of the Navy, and Department of the Air Force. A four-star general (most senior commander) heads each major command. Commands have numbered air forces (Naifs) or air divisions (Ads).

There are six commands. The two commands that concern fighter pilots are the air training command at Randolph AFB, Texas, and the air combat command at Largely AFB, Virginia.

Nearly all airmen and officers are trained in some way at Randolph AFB. All fighter pilots are commanded by the air combat command at Largely AFB, Virginia.

The air combat command has wings, groups, squadrons, and flights. These are units of pilots and fighter planes. Wings have the most number of planes and pilots. Flights have the fewest number of planes and pilots.

FIGHTER PILOT GROUPS

The squadron is the building block of the command. A fighter squadron has eighteen to twenty-four fighter planes. Four or more squadrons are in a wing.

The basic fighting unit of the Air Force is the wing. A wing is stationed at an Air Force base. The wing may have only one type of aircraft, such as fighters, or it may be a composite (more than one type of aircraft) wing. A composite wing may have fighters, fighter bombers, and stealth aircraft.

For example, the 16th Air Force is headquartered at Aviano Air Base, Italy. It has two wings and one group. Because stealth aircraft have limited range, they may be based at a forward (close to the battlefront) airfield. In that case, fighter planes are needed to protect the stealth planes from enemy air attacks.

Fighter Pilot Training

INTRODUCTORY FLIGHT TRAINING (IFT)

Officers entering the Air Force pilot training program without a private pilot license (PPL) must go through introductory flight training (IFT). Air Force Academy cadets and Air Force lieutenants who live in an area near the Academy will take their training at the Air Force Academy. All others will go to the Air Force officer accession and training schools (AFOATS) located at Maxwell Air Force Base, Alabama.

The purpose of IFT is to reduce the dropout rate during the specialized undergraduate pilot training (SUPT) course. Students who already have a PPL or higher are required to fly with an FAA-certified flight instructor. The instructor

Air Force Academy cadets learn how to behave in a military manner.

gives the student a flight review. This review tests a pilot's takeoff, flying, and landing abilities.

A certified civilian contractor gives all introductory flight training. The Air Force pays for a total of 50 hours of flying time. Students must fly solo (without a teacher present) before reaching 25 hours of instruction. Students also must qualify for a private pilot license. The Air Force pays for any required equipment or materials, and for the necessary FAA Class III physical. This physical tests a person's general health and eyesight.

SPECIALIZED UNDERGRADUATE PILOT TRAINING (SUPT)

SUPT is a fifty-three-week course that teaches officers to be Air Force pilots. It's given at Columbus AFB in Columbus, Mississippi, and at Laughlin AFB in Del Rio, Texas.

For the first six months, officers fly the T-37 Tweet. It's a twin-engine jet trainer. Trainees sit

The T-37 is a trainer jet.

side-by-side with an instructor. The instructor watches every move the trainee makes. The instructor also can take control of the aircraft in an emergency. This system of instruction ensures safety. It also is a hands-on way for an instructor to test whether a trainee will make a good Air Force fighter pilot!

Trainees fly the T-38 Talon during the last six months of training. The T-38 is much faster and more sophisticated than the T-37. Seating is front and back, just like in planes that trained pilots fly. Trainees sit on a rocket-powered ejection seat in a pressurized, air-conditioned cockpit. This aircraft can climb from sea level to about 30,000 feet in one minute. That's a little like riding atop a rocket. Mastery of this aircraft prepares trainees to fly the F-15, F-16, A-10, and F-111.

The T-38 (right) is the next step during flight school.

Fighter Pilots in the Sky

Air Force fighter pilots are stationed around the world. Pilots live on air force bases. These are small communities centered around an airport. Air force bases have apartments, houses, stores, and office buildings. Unmarried pilots live on base in dormitories. Married officers can live on base or off base.

Life is centered on training, unless a pilot is sent into action. When called to action, pilots are already in the proper frame of mind because of the training they receive. The type of flying each fighter pilot performs teaches him how to manage his fear.

Management of fear starts with realistic training. The most realistic fighter pilot training in the world takes place at Nellis Air Force Base, Nevada. Fighter pilots are sent to Nellis to

The F-111 Raven is one of four fighter jets the Air Force uses during battle.

participate in Red Flag. Red Flag is a training program that teaches fighting tactics.

At Nellis, experienced pilots are used to train all fighter pilots coming through the program. These experienced pilots disguise themselves as an enemy air force. They wear Russian-style uniforms, fly fighter planes with Russian-style camouflage and markings, and use Russian tactics to shoot down American fighter pilots. They usually succeed. Their purpose is to teach real tactics that U.S. Air Force pilots will encounter in real combat situations. Russian-style jets and tactics are used because most enemy fighter pilots have been trained by the former Soviet Union.

Historical records show that most fighter pilots killed in action are killed during their first ten combat missions. The training concept at Nellis is to give fighter pilots their first ten combat missions without actually killing them. This training uses real flying tactics and simulated weapons fire. Weapons can be simulated to fire against a jet fighter using electronic sensors. These sensors are placed on the trainee's jet fighter and the "enemy" jet fighter. Each plane also has infrared (high-beam) light beams that can be shot at a plane. If the infrared light beam hits a sensor on the jet fighter, that fighter has been "hit" and is considered shot down. These electronic light beams and sensors allow trainees to experience real combat flying and battle without actually being in danger of real missiles and cannon fire killing them.

While flying Red Flag simulated battles, fighter pilot trainees always know they are going to fly against an enemy aircraft. However, they never know where or when. When the air battle happens, it's always a heart-stopping surprise! On being jumped by Red Flag aggressors, friendlies dive, maneuver, and soar in an attempt to come around and turn the tables on their attackers. They practice their dogfighting skills as though it were a real fight. Sometimes their skills work. But more often than not, the aggressor is the one who wins the "battle."

Pilots all agree that the training at Nellis is the most valuable of all.

HOT SPOTS IN THE WORLD

In between such specialized training as Red Flag, fighter pilots fly missions in different parts of the world. These places are called "hot spots." They are called hot spots because battles could take place in such places. Usually these are areas where unfriendly countries must be watched by U.S. military forces. The U.S. Air Force is a perfect tool to carry out such missions. Fighter pilots have the ability to fly long distances. They can gather information about enemy stations or movements and return home quickly.

Fighter pilots also serve as a show of force. An enemy is unlikely to cause trouble if it knows that a high-tech weapon like an F-16 is in the area. This is because the F-16 has the ability to destroy almost anything that comes up against it. Hot spots today include Iraq (Middle East) and the Balkan nation of Yugoslavia (Europe). The rulers of these nations

This F-16B fighting Falcon can fire missiles at enemy planes.

have proved that they are dangerous. Because the United States is the most powerful nation in the world, it has special duties. The Air Force uses its pilots to help control these nations. They do so by flying patrol missions both near and in these nations. Such patrols help to keep these nations in check.

Air Force fighter pilots don't want to fight and kill, but they have been trained to do so. They will fight an enemy if that enemy shoots first.

FIGHTER PILOT JETS

F-15, F-16, and A-10

Air Force fighter pilots fly the F-15, F-16, A-10, and several other jets. These fighter planes are used for a variety of different missions. The F-15 and F-16 are fighter and bomber jets. They have the ability to fight other jets in the sky. These jets have special radar (electronic search systems) that can detect other planes in the air. This radar tracks an enemy plane. When the F-15 or F-16 gets close enough to the enemy, its radar locks onto the enemy plane. Then the pilot can fire a missile at the enemy. Often, an enemy knows it's being chased because it has its own radar. When an enemy knows a U.S. Air Force fighter jet is there, it usually flies away.

These fighter jets also can make contact with a ground target and destroy it using bombs that the jets carry. The F-15 and F-16 planes use a type of radar that is just for

This F-15 pilot sits beneath a fiberglass canopy.

31

detecting ground targets. This radar can find an enemy radar station that is looking for the jet fighter. Using radar homing (seeking) missiles, the fighter pilot can destroy the radar station so that the enemy won't locate the jet fighter.

The A-10 is known as the Warthog. The Warthog got its name because it flies so low to the ground that it looks as if its nose can burrow into the earth at any moment. The Warthog is used mostly against enemy tanks. Tanks are slow-moving compared to a jet fighter. The A-10 Warthog was designed so that it can fly at very low speeds. This ability makes it a great threat against tanks. Its radar helps it to locate tanks and other ground targets. Its rockets and missiles are suited to hit such slow-moving or fixed targets.

FIGHTER PILOT WEAPONS

AIM-9 Sidewinder

The Sidewinder is an air-to-air missile that is used against another flying airplane. The Sidewinder works by sensing the heat from an enemy plane's engine exhaust. Its heat-seeking ability allows it to locate its target without further guidance from the pilot. That means the jet fighter can leave an area once it fires the

Pilots check their planes and weapons before each mission.

weapon at its target. The Sidewinder has a range (flying distance) of 10 miles.

AGM–88 HARM

The Harm missile is used against enemy radar stations. It seeks out ground-based stations by homing in on the radiation signals that stations use to detect planes in the sky. Once the Harm missile has tracked a station, it flies straight at it and explodes on impact. The Harm missile has a range of more than 30 miles.

AIM-120 AMRAAM

The AIM-120 advanced medium range air-to-air missile is a newer weapon. It is a better missile than the AIM-9 because it can be used in all weather and from longer distances. The AMRAAM has an active radar system. This means that once it is close to its target, it closes in on the target no matter where that target turns. The AMRAAM has a range of more than 20 miles.

The AIM-120 AMRAAM missile is used against enemy targets that use radar.

AGM-65 Maverick

The Maverick is a video-aimed missile used against ground targets. Inside the cockpit (pilot seat), the fighter pilot aims the missile by locating the target on a video screen. Once the target is pinpointed, the pilot shoots the Maverick. The Maverick guides itself to the target and explodes on impact. As many as six Maverick missiles can be carried by either the A-10, F-15, or F-16. Its range is nearly 15 miles.

GBU-15

The GBU-15 (guided bomb unit) is a bomb that glides its way to a ground target. The GBU-15 has a television guiding system for daytime use. It has an infrared imaging (night-seeing electronics) system for night use. The pilot drops this bomb while flying near its target. If the pilot is flying at a high altitude (height), the GBU–15 can be dropped nearly 15 miles from its target. At lower altitudes, the pilot can be as close as 5 miles (the closest a pilot wants to

Many fighter planes can carry as many as six Maverick missiles.

come to a guarded target) from the target. Once the bomb is dropped, the pilot can leave the area and guide the weapon to its target using a video screen.

The Future Of FighterPilots

Flight simulators are commonly in use today. They allow pilots to practice takeoffs, landings, and cross-country flying under realistic conditions. Flight simulators use computer flight programs. Even emergency situations such as engine failures, fire, and instrument malfunctions are easily simulated. Simulated emergencies provide pilots with valuable training in handling routine in-flight problems. Such training is often a matter of life and death. Also, it's much cheaper and far less dangerous than setting up such emergencies using real aircraft.

Training for such emergencies using real jet aircraft is too expensive.

Today, computers are changing even that. All jet fighter pilots "fly" hundreds of hours on computer-based flight programs.

The F-22 Raptor will someday replace the F-16. The Raptor is able to escape enemy radar.

High-tech flight simulators are special machines. Their combination of mechanical and computerized equipment has been keeping fighter pilots "fresh" for many years. As flight simulators become more realistic, Air Force pilots will become more easily trained for combat missions.

HOW THE AIR FORCE WILL BE USED

Today's world is changing as fast as its computers. There are many countries still looking to fight one another. Such hot spots need to be observed. The best way to do this job is through constant watch by Air Force jets. These jets allow quick entrance and exit from enemy territory. They also offer superior firepower if a battle heats up.

If a war does start, the Air Force is a more efficient fighting machine than are ground troops. Fighter jets have tons of bombs at hand, and only one person is in harm's way—

Military aircraft engineers are always designing new and better jet fighters.

the pilot. Ground troops need thousands of men to fight a battle, and many of them can die. The odds are better to use a fast jet equipped with high-tech weapons and the ability to destroy an enemy target from a long distance.

FASTER PLANES AND BETTER WEAPONS

The F-22 Raptor is a jet fighter that will replace the F-16. It is now in its middle stages of testing. The Raptor will be faster, use less fuel, and have quicker moves than any jet fighter made. Add that to a long list of newer and better missiles and bombs. The F-22 Raptor with its high-tech weapons will be a jet fighter that any Air Force fighter pilot will want to fly!

41

New Words

air force base where pilots live

air-to-air missile a rocket bomb used to shoot from one airplane at another

allied countries friendly to the United States

altitude height

dogfights air battles during which fighter planes circle each other closely

flight simulators computers that let pilots practice flying skills, through using video screens

homing missiles rocket bombs that use radar (electronic search device) to find their targets

hot spots places in the world where battles or wars may easily happen

New Words

infrared imaging system electronic system
used to find enemy targets in the dark

operations duties

radar (RAdio Detecting And Ranging) using
radio waves to locate objects

reserve commission held back for an emergency

squadrons group of eighteen to twenty-four
fighter planes

tactics ways of fighting

wing basic fighting unit of the Air Force,
made up of four or more squadrons

For Further Reading

Blue, Rose and Corrine J. Naden. *The U.S. Air Force.* Brookfield, CT: Millbrook Press, 1994.

Covert, Kim. *U.S. Air Force Special Forces Combat Controllers: Combat Controllers.* Danbury, CT: Franklin Watts, 1999.

Ferrell, Nancy W. *The U.S. Air Force.* Minneapolis, MN: The Lerner Publishing Group, 1990.

Hole, Dorothy. *The Air Force and You.* Parsippany, NJ: Silver Burdett Press, 1993.

Resources

Air Force Link

www.af.mil

This is the official site of the U.S. Air Force. Learn more about the Air Force and the different careers that are available. This site includes pictures, current news, and a library.

Air Force Reserve–Above and Beyond

www.afreserve.com/priorservice

This site explains the benefits of serving in the Air Force Reserve. It contains information about what is required and the commitment that is necessary to join. This site also allows you to contact a recruiter.

Resources

United States Air Force Museum
1100 Spaatz Street
Wright-Patterson AFB, OH 45433
(937) 255-3286
Web site: *www.wpafb.af.mil/museum*
The United States Air Force Museum is dedicated to documenting the history of the Air Force. This museum has more than three hundred missiles and aircraft on display. It also has various tours, exhibits, and lectures.

Index

Index

About the Author

Robert C. Kennedy entered the U.S. Army at age seventeen and attended various specialized schools. He served with a military intelligence detachment during the Korean War and with a special operations detachment during the Vietnam War, in 1967. He ended his career as an instructor for the Military Intelligence Officer Advanced Course, which he helped to develop, in 1968.